OPENING CLOSURES

A Young Mother's Dying Declarations

Edited by
by B. Elwin Sherman

Fractal Interpretations by
B. Z. Leonard

© 2007 by B. Elwin Sherman

All rights reserved. No part of this book may be reproduced, stored in a retrieval system or transmitted in any form or by any means without the prior written permission of the author or illustrator, except by a reviewer who may quote brief passages in a review for print media or internet newspapers, magazines or journals.

ISBN: 978-0-6151-6864-7
First Edition   First Printing

Other Books By The Author:

GEORGE W. BUSH -- *On The Trips Of His Tongue -- A Linguistic Legacy*

CAUGHT IN THE SHOWER WITHOUT A PENCIL -- *Baby Boomer Humor, And Other Maturity Problems*

HumorUs -- (With The NetWits)

THE MIRADORS -- *Descensions Of A Man*

TOOLKIT IN PARADISE -- *The Self-Helpless Guide To A Decade Of American Wit & Wisdom*

B. Elwin Sherman's Website: elwinshumor.com
B.Z. Leonard's Website: art-bzl.com

Dr. Elisabeth Kübler-Ross quotation used with permission. Elisabeth Kübler-Ross Foundation.
Please visit them at: elisabethkublerross.com and ekrfoundation.org

Front Cover Art: "Mad Plaid Swirl" by B.Z. Leonard

"Hospice Family Care, Inc." logo used with permission. Contact: hfc-az.com

* * *

Designed by B. Elwin Sherman

Manufactured in the United States of America

For information regarding special discounts for bulk purchases,
please contact the author/publisher at:

P.O. Box 360
Bethlehem, NH 03574
USA

DEDICATION:

To all who attend the passings.

* * *

EDITOR'S PREFACE

Vicki lived and died.

Her worldly station was commonly grounded in the domestic American landscape. She was a good mother to her two children, Erin and Jessie, and a devoted wife to her husband Richard. She lived for thirty-five years, then she died.

She was neither crowned nor canonized. Her wealth, power and notoriety came in her love of family and friends, and in an abiding celebration of life itself.

She attended PTA meetings, put out the dog, mended overalls, tended houseplants, closed the windows when it rained, and pre-soaked tablecloths. She loved oranges. She was most comfortable wearing shorts and a t-shirt. She was a sucker for sappy love stories.

Vicki balanced the checkbooks, filed the tax returns, paid off the installment loan on the washer & dryer, and stayed up all night holding the buckets when Erin & Jessie brought home an intestinal flu.

She cried at weddings and laughed at my jokes.

She wrote poetry in the dark, and never could decide whether her kindred musical spirit was Janis Joplin or Loretta Lynn.

She was a harbor for the quietly desperate passion we all rarely acknowledge, but ring in with every sunrise. In the earthly scheme of things she was known only to a few, but was everyone's good neighbor.

Vicki was my hospice patient, and I was there to help her and her family tend her life as she faced its untimely end from a terrible cancer.

During a visit with Vicki at her home a month before she died, she handed me a letter and asked if I would someday see that its contents were published.

This book is as simple as that.

Here are those courageous young mother's last written words of departure, made visual by the fractal imagery of renowned artist B.Z. Leonard.

Read the words. Look at the pictures. Make the connections.

Celebrate life.

B. Elwin Sherman
Autumn 2007

List Of Illustrations

The Maw 15
YinYang 17
The Theater 19
Caldera 21
Enigma 23
Ribbonesque 25
Fusing 27
Hesitating Talisman 29
Raybans 31
Red Tide 33
Blue Flower 35
Legacy 37
Spring Song 39
Pinnacled Perception 41
Ribbonned Galaxies 43

The Big Bang 45
Interstitiality 47
Sunrise Sunset 49
Sharp Dilemma 51
Spawnee 53
Triskelion 55
Red Drip 57
Coral Reach 59
Fall Leaves 61
Mixer 63
Birth 65
Ball Drop 67
Mad Plaid Swirl 69
Golden Cleave 71

OPENING CLOSURES

*"... People are like stained-glass windows.
They sparkle and shine when the sun is out,
but when the darkness sets in,
their true beauty is revealed only if there is a light from within."*

--- Dr. Elisabeth Kübler-Ross ---

To my dear family and friends:

My time on earth has not been easy.
But, looking at it now,
I can see the reasons.

The ups and downs, the pain and joy,
all had a purpose.

I have not lived in vain.

Because of my trials,
I have really been alive.

I have felt the depths of happiness and suffering that most cannot imagine.

Each experience was met in the moment.

Each moment was experienced to the end.

There was no going with the flow,
or turning of the head.

I approached it all with my eyes wide open.

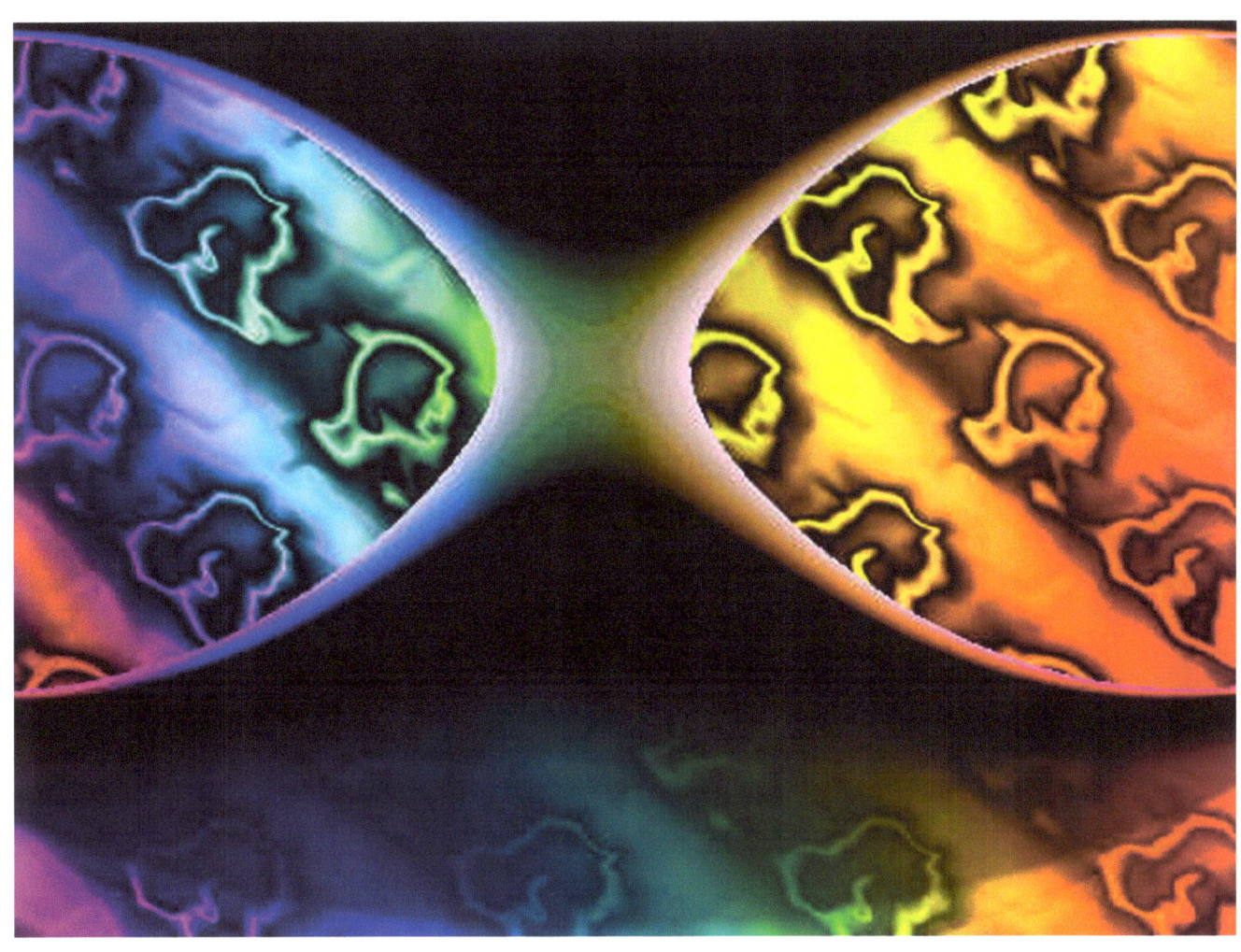

So, as I leave, do not be sad.
This was one life that had true meaning.

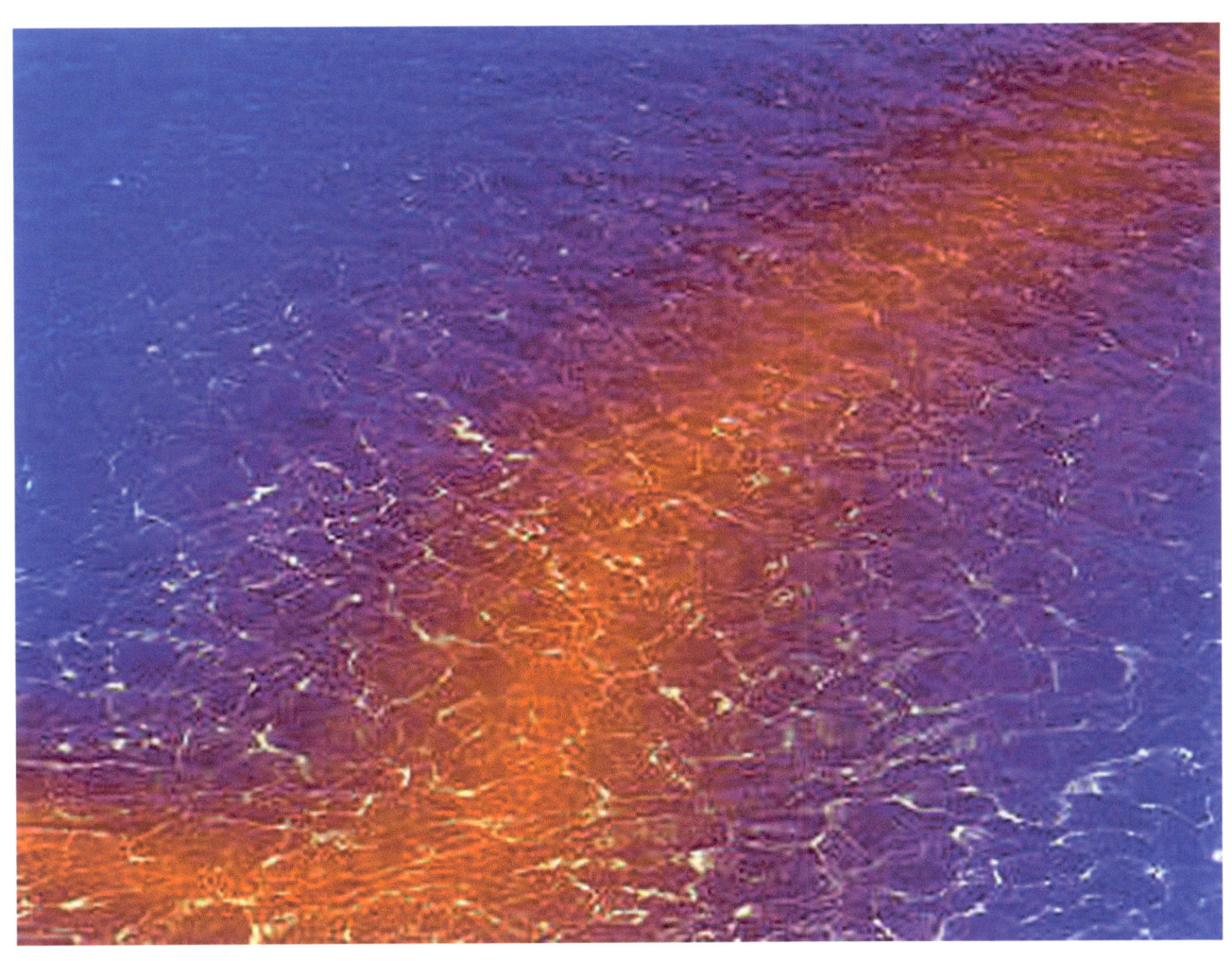

I hope that by my actions and reactions
I have been a guide here, a kind of teacher
for the rough times.

I hope you can somehow feel enriched
by our lives crossing, as I certainly do.

Each relationship and embrace,
every angry or kind word spoken,
left me richer by all measures.

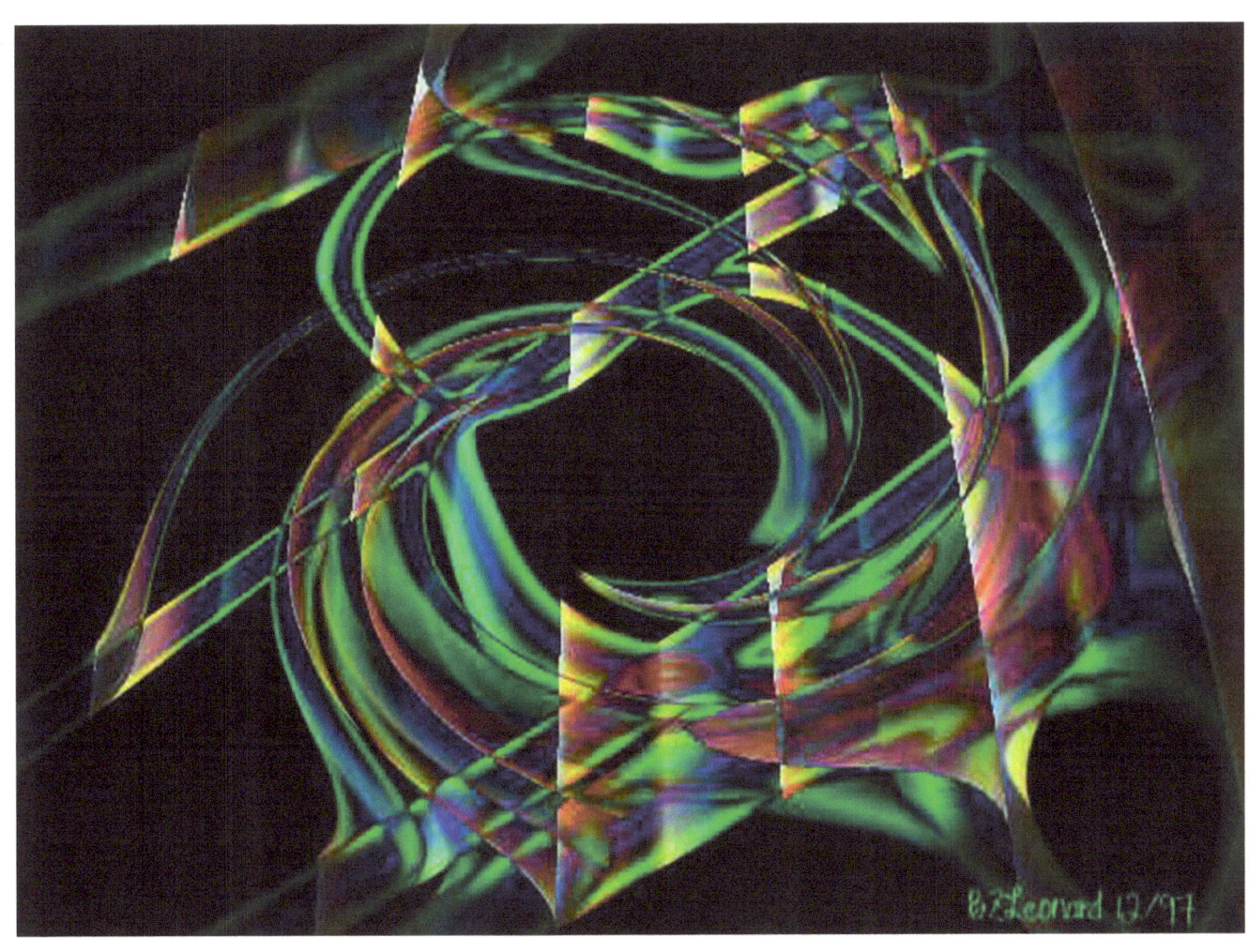

I have seen compassion at its highest level
and cruelty at its lowest point.
But, do not feel sorry for the latter.
It is only by that as a guideline
that the true depth of my blessings
became clear.

To those whom I have loved,
and to those who have loved me,
I say: thank you.

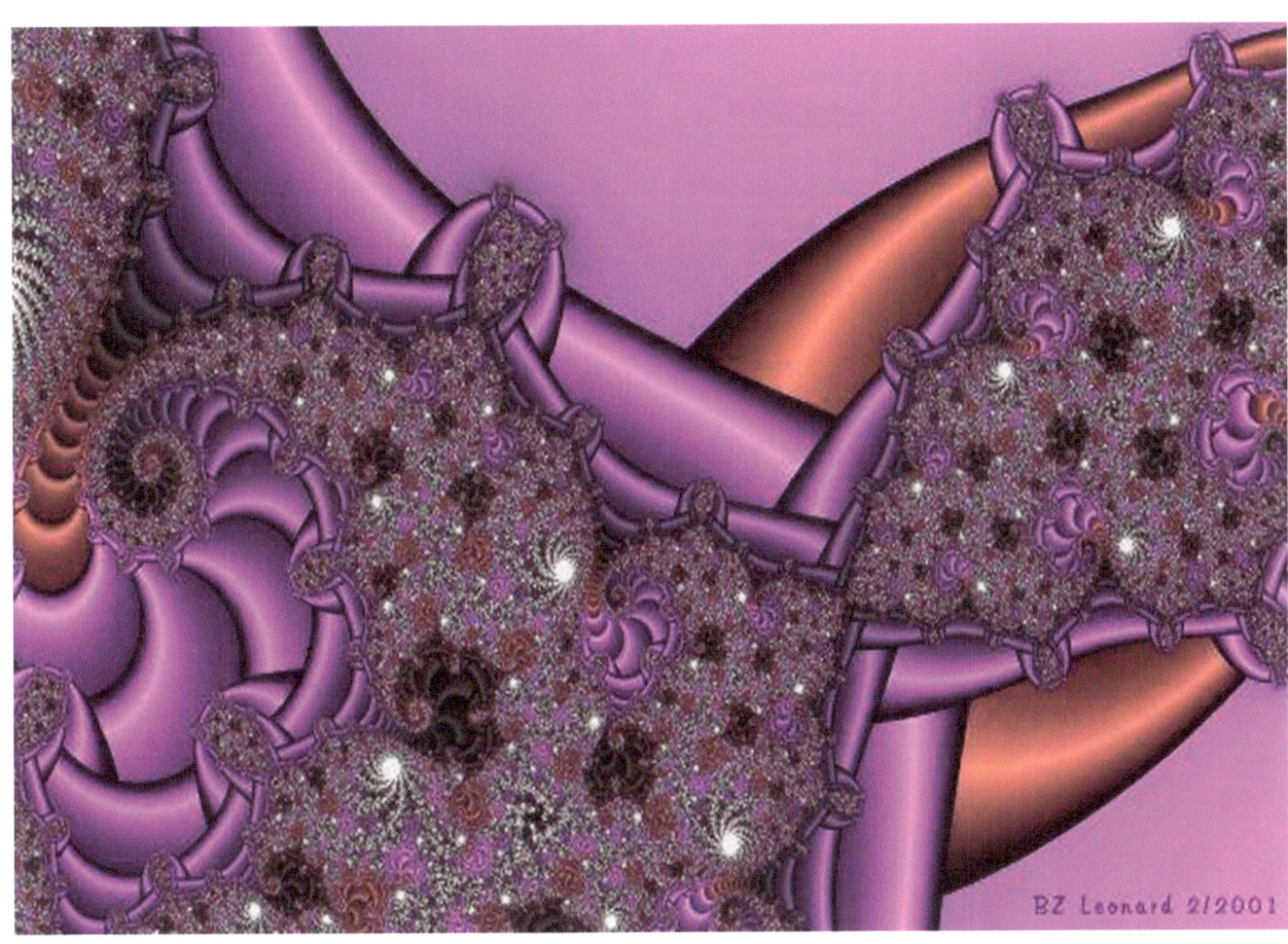

You have been my peace, my comfort, my source of strength.

And, to those with whom I shared some "not so perfect" times, I want to say
I am sorry.

Please know
that I never had a forethought of malice,
but was guilty of stubbornness
and too much pride.

I always felt a strong sense of loss
when a relationship didn't work out.

My good intentions did not always show through, much to my sadness.

To all of you,
be proud of the role that you had
in making my life.

Thank you for our precious time together.
I would not change a thing.

All the ups and downs,
bumps and smooth sailing,
made life sweeter and more precious.

It is difficult to understand
why God has to take me so soon,
when I feel my work here is far from complete.

But, I'm sure He will watch over
what is to come in my place.

I know that He has a plan for me,
and I pray to be worthy of my tasks
that lie ahead.

If mourn you must,
let it pass quickly.

Many tears were shed during my life.
Let my death be the end of that,
and the beginning of a search
for all the love, joy and peace
this life has to hold.

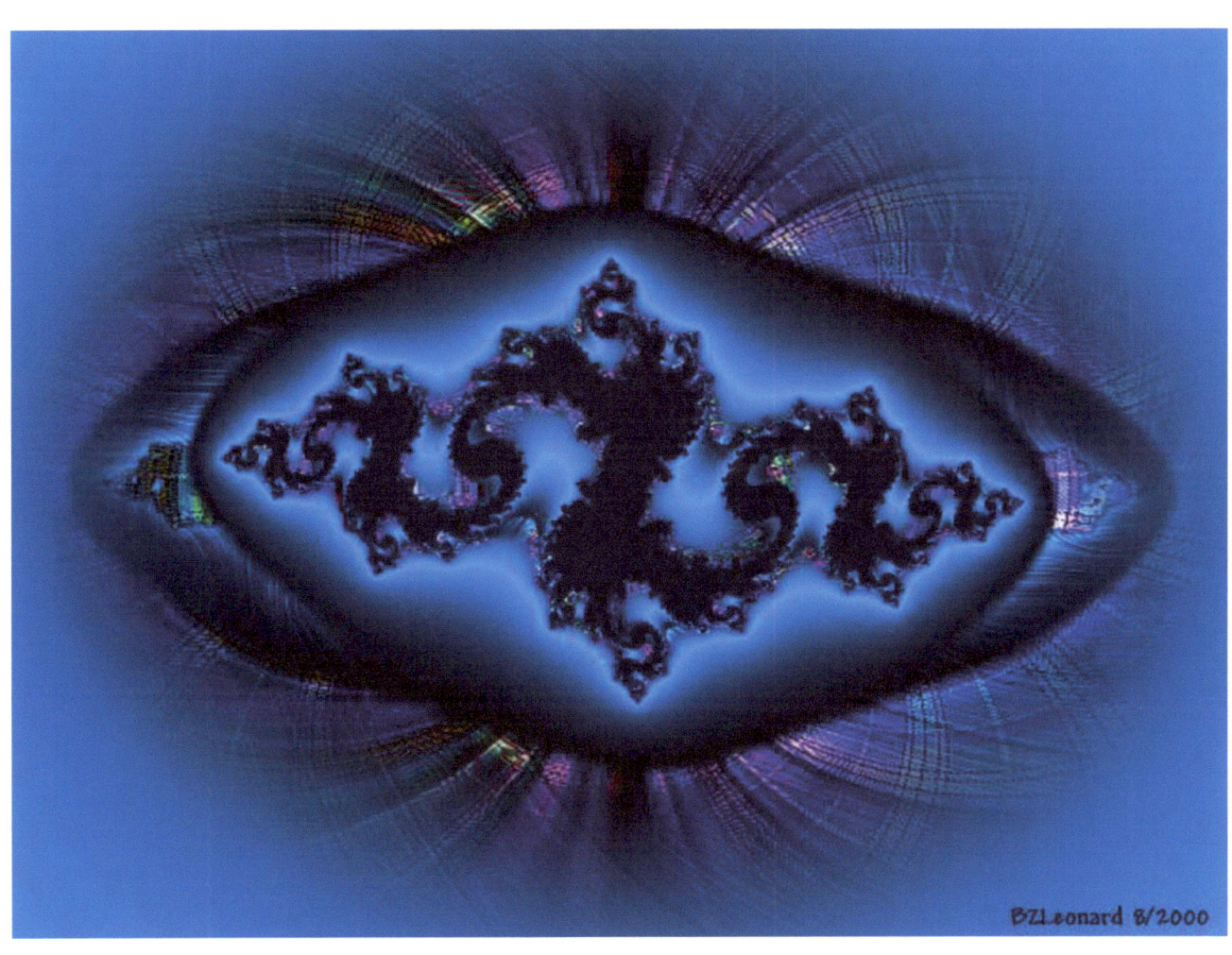

Always with you,
Vicki

Vicki died one month later, with Erin, Jessie and Richard at her bedside.

Her funeral procession to a remote Southwestern desert gravesite went largely unnoticed, though something in all of us everywhere stood back and watched the coffin pass.

We wouldn't have missed her --- for the world.

B. Elwin Sherman
B. Z. Leonard

* * * * *

www.ingramcontent.com/pod-product-compliance
Lightning Source LLC
Chambersburg PA
CBHW041529220426
43671CB00002B/32